CRACKING THE PARENT CODE: A FUN GUIDE FOR KIDS

By: Brenda D. Proctor
Cover & Book Design: Aaron C. Butler, Nalani Butler

ISBN: 9781967082605
Library of Congress Control Number: 2025923480

Printed in the United States of America

BookButler Publishing Company
Upper Marlboro, MD 20774

TheBookButler.com

PUBLISHING COMPANY

Table of Contents

Introduction 1

Word bank 6

Match the Emotion 17

Feelings in Disguise 22

Rules Rules Rules 28

How to Hear More 34

Parents Were Once Kids Too 39

Cracking the Love Code 44

When Grown-Ups Mess Up................................. 50

You Can Be a Mind Reader (Sort of) 55

Final Mission 61

Mission Debrief 68

ARE GROWN-UPS JUST
BIG KIDS?

Have you ever looked at your mom, dad, or teacher and thought, "Why are they acting like that?" Maybe they got mad about a missing sock. Maybe they sighed out loud over bills. Or maybe they said "no" to something fun for what felt like no reason at all.

Guess what? Even though grown-ups are taller (and way busier), they're still people–just like you! They get scared, make mistakes, and even dream about their future.

Here's the difference: their brains are juggling tons of stuff–like work, bills, laundry, cooking, cleaning, and YOU. Imagine your brain trying to carry a backpack that's stuffed full. That's how a parent's brain feels most of the time!

That's why I wrote **Cracking the Parent Code: A Fun Guide for Kids.** It's your secret decoder for understanding the mysterious world of grown-ups. You'll learn why they say the things they do, spot the hidden feelings behind their moods, and even figure out how to work together better—as one awesome family team.

Ready? Let's dive in and start cracking the parent code!

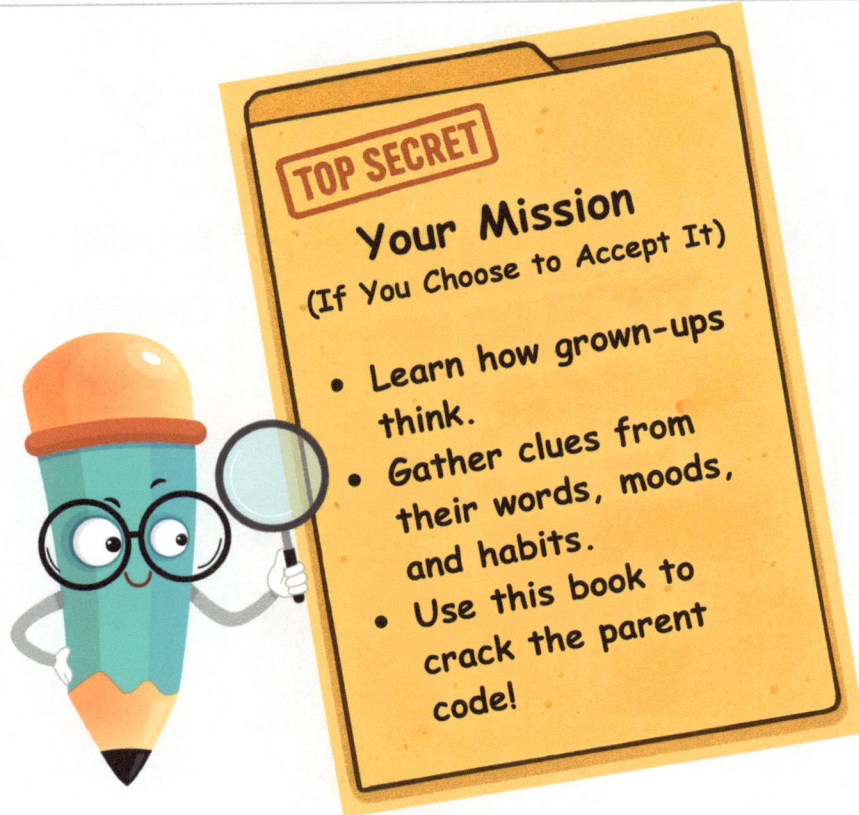

TOP SECRET

Your Mission
(If You Choose to Accept It)

- Learn how grown-ups think.
- Gather clues from their words, moods, and habits.
- Use this book to crack the parent code!

YOUR CODE CRACKER ID

Before you can take on your first mission, you need to gear up like a real detective. Every spy starts with an official **Agent-in-Training ID** to prove they're on the case. This one is yours!

Fill it out, decorate it, and keep it handy – you'll be earning special badges throughout the book as you complete each mission. By the end, your ID will show you've leveled up to a full **Master Code Cracker!**

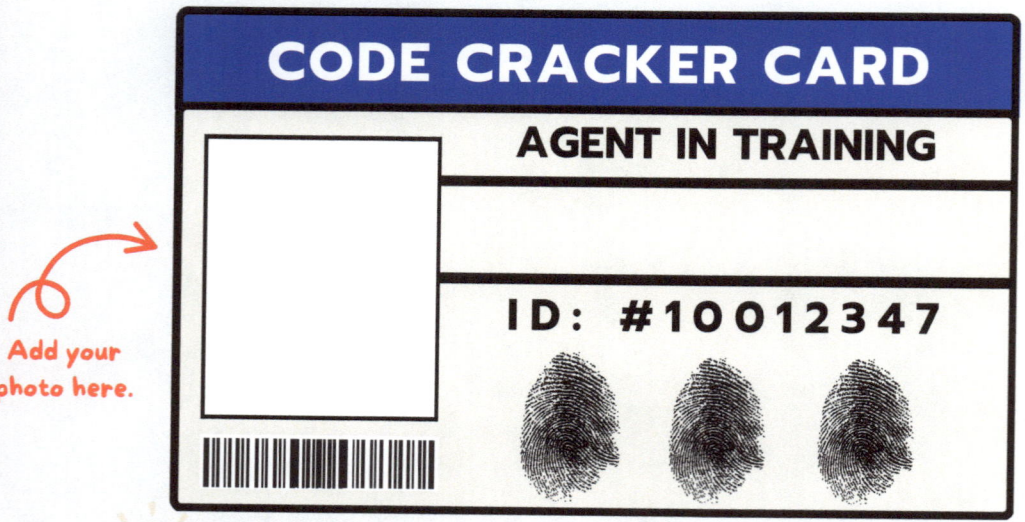

CODE CRACKER CARD

AGENT IN TRAINING

ID: #10012347

Add your photo here.

Add your name here.

💡 **Spy Tip:** Keep your badge handy – you'll need it for every mission in this book.

CRACK THE PARENT CODE QUIZ

Before we dive in, let's have some fun. Think of this as your very first mission: figure out what type of grown-up you're dealing with. Choose the answer that sounds most like your parent, grandparent, or teacher.

No wrong answers – just clues to help you crack their code!

When something goes wrong, they...

A. Shrug and say, "Oh well!"

B. Rub their forehead and stare into space.

C. Look around for someone or something to blame.

Their favorite phrase is...

A. "Because I said so."

B. "Not right now."

C. "Go read a book."

They act most like a kid when...

A. A dog is around (instant silly mode!).

B. They tell a joke and laugh harder than anyone.

C. They dance when they think no one is watching.

If they had a superhero name, it would be...

A. Captain Checklist

B. The Worry Wizard

C. The Napping Ninja

NOW CRACK THE CODE!

Mostly A's ➡ **The Rule Follower**

Your grown-up likes structure, lists, and doing things the "right way." But watch out — under that serious side, there's a secret silly streak waiting to pop out.

Mostly B's ➡ **The Daydreamer**

Your grown-up is thoughtful and caring, but their brain is juggling a million things at once. Sometimes they zone out, but it's usually because they're solving problems in their head.

Mostly C's ➡ **The Kid-at-Heart**

Your grown-up might actually be one of the biggest kids in the house! They laugh hard, dance goofy, and love having fun. (Just don't tell them you figured out their secret.)

CODE CRACKER'S WORD BANK

Before you can crack the parent code, you need the right tools. Think of these words as the secret gadgets in your detective kit. Each one helps you understand the mysterious world of grown-ups a little better.

Don't worry – they may sound big at first, but I'll break them down into examples you already know. Once you understand these words, you'll be able to explain feelings and behavior like a pro.

Get ready to think like a super sleuth!

Aggression - When someone acts mean or is ready to fight.

➡️ *Example: Pushing in front of someone to grab the swing first.*

Anxiety - That nervous, butterfly-in-the-stomach feeling.

➡️ *Example: Standing backstage before the school play.*

Attachment - A special bond or connection you feel with someone you love.

➡️ *Example: Feeling safe and happy when your grandma hugs you.*

Behavior - What someone does and how they act.

➡️ *Example: Sharing your toys is kind behavior. Yelling at your friend is unkind behavior.*

Bias - When you like or dislike something more than is fair.

➡️ *Example: Always picking your best friend for dodgeball, even if someone else throws better.*

Consciousness - Knowing your own thoughts and feelings.

➡️ *Example: Realizing you're cranky because you skipped lunch.*

Delusion - Believing something that isn't true.

➡️ *Example: Thinking you can fly by flapping your arms.*

Depression - Feeling very sad for a long time and losing interest in fun things.

➡️ *Example: Not wanting to play your favorite video game for weeks because you feel down.*

Ego - The part of your mind that balances what you want with what's right.

→ *Example: Wanting to eat all the cookies but knowing you should leave some for others.*

Emotional Intelligence - Understanding and handling feelings well.

→ *Example: Noticing your friend is upset and cheering them up.*

Extrovert - Someone who feels energized by being around lots of people.

→ *Example: Grabbing the mic first at karaoke night.*

Influence - The power to change how someone thinks or acts.

→ *Example: Your friend gets a cool hat – suddenly, you want one too.*

Introvert - Someone who enjoys being alone or in small groups.

→ *Example: Reading in your room instead of going to a big party.*

Optimistic - Believing good things will happen.

➡️ *Example: Thinking it'll be sunny tomorrow even though it's cloudy now.*

Pacifist - Someone who believes fighting is wrong.

➡️ *Example: Solving an argument with words instead of punches.*

Perception - The way you understand what you see, hear, or feel.

➡️ *Example: Two kids see the same cloud – one sees a dog, the other sees a dragon.*

Personality - The special way you usually think, feel, and act.

➡️ *Example: Being the class clown who always makes people laugh.*

Pessimistic - Expecting bad things to happen.

➡️ *Example: Thinking your soccer game will be canceled because of one tiny raincloud.*

Phobia - A very strong fear of something.

➡️ *Example: Screaming when you see a harmless spider.*

Psychology - The science of how people think, feel, and act.

➡️ *Example: Studying why kids laugh more than adults.*

Self-Esteem - How much you believe in yourself and know you are valuable.

➡️ *Example: Looking in the mirror and thinking, "I'm awesome just the way I am."*

Social Psychology - How people affect each other.

➡️ *Example: One kid's laugh makes the class laugh.*

Stress - Feeling tense because of problems or challenges.

Example: Worrying about finishing a big homework project on time.

Therapy - Talking to someone trained to help you feel better.

➡️ *Example: Meeting with a counselor when you feel sad.*

Trauma - Something very upsetting or scary that happens.

➡️ *Example: Feeling shaken for a long time after a car accident.*

W	O	
	R	D

THE CODE CRACKER GAME

Now that you've loaded up your secret word bank, it's time to test your detective skills! Can you match the tricky psychology words with their true meanings? *Grab some index cards and a friend, and let's play...*

How to Set Up Your Mission:

1. Write one word from the Word Bank on a card.

2. On a separate card, write its matching definition.

3. Keep going until you've got a whole deck of words and meanings.

Now shuffle your cards – the code is scrambled!

How to Play:

1. Place the word cards face down on the table in rows.

2. Keep the definition cards stacked in a pile.

3. On your turn, draw a definition card and read it out loud.

4. Pick a word card from the rows and flip it over.

   • If it matches, you cracked the code! Keep the pair and take another turn.

   • If it doesn't, flip the card back over. The next detective takes a turn.

5. Keep playing until all the codes are solved.

Winning the Mission:

The player with the most word pairs at the end of the game wins!

WHAT ARE PARENTS THINKING?

MISSION BRIEFING

Have you ever stared at your parent and wondered, "What's going on in their head right now?" Maybe they're staring into space. Maybe they're sighing. Maybe they're grumpy for no reason.

Here's the truth: grown-up brains are BUSY. They're juggling about a zillion things at once – like a giant snow globe swirling with to-do lists, worry clouds, and love bubbles.

 Your mission in this chapter: **crack the mystery of what parents think about all day.**

CHAPTER 1

CLUES & EVIDENCE

Let's compare your brain to your parent's brain.

KID TO-DO LIST

- Go to school
- Do homework
- Feed the pet
- Clean your room (sometimes)
- Have fun!

PARENT TO-DO LIST

- Go to work (all day)
- Pay bills
- Shop for groceries
- Cook meals
- Do laundry
- Drive everyone everywhere
- Take care of you when you're sick
- Remember EVERYTHING (doctor appointments, birthdays, permission slips, etc.)
- AND MORE.....

See the difference? While you're thinking about playing outside, your parent might be thinking about dinner, the electric bill, and making sure you brushed your teeth.

What Are Worry Clouds?

Worry Clouds are the little thoughts that float through a parent's brain and make them nervous or stressed. They might wonder, "Will I have enough money this month?" or "Is my kid safe at school?"

When too many Worry Clouds pile up, it can make parents snap, sigh, or look distracted.

What Are Love Bubbles?

Love Bubbles are the happy thoughts that pop every time parents think about how much they love you. They show up when they watch you blow out birthday candles, smile at your artwork, or cheer when you learn something new.

Even if they don't say it out loud, Love Bubbles are ALWAYS floating around in their minds – sparkling, just for you.

TOP SECRET

YOUR MISSION: Decode the Parent Brain!

Imagine your parent's brain is a snow globe. Inside it are:

- To-Do Lists (school lunches, work stuff, laundry, bills)
- Worry Clouds (safety, money, "Will my kid be okay?")
- Love Bubbles (smiling when you do something new, cheering for you, caring about you always)

Activity: Inside the snow globe, write or doodle the things you think swirl around in your parent's brain every day. Be sure to add a few Love Bubbles — they're always there, even if you can't see them!

Spy Tip: Parents' brains may look stormy on the outside, but inside, there are always Love Bubbles floating around for YOU.

MISSION:
MATCH THE EMOTION

 **MISSION BRIEFING**

A great detective doesn't just listen to words – they watch faces and body language. Parents don't always say what they're feeling, but their expressions often give them away. Your mission is to learn how to spot the clues!

 **CLUES & EVIDENCE**

Here's the secret: every face makes tiny "emotion codes" when someone feels something big. A raised eyebrow, a wrinkled forehead, or a big grin – these are clues detectives use to figure out the truth.

CASE FILE ACTIVITY:
DECODE THE FACES

Match each facial expression to the correct emotion from the list.

Spy Tip: Every detective knows: people can say one thing but their face tells the real story. If your parent says "I'm fine" but their face looks worried, that's your clue to look for a Worry Cloud.

 ● ● Tired

 ● ● Happy

 ● ● Angry

 ● ● Sick

 ● ● Frightened

 ● ● Worried

 ● ● Sad

SPY DRILL TRAINING
KNOW YOURSELF FIRST

Every great detective has to practice reading their own feelings before they can decode someone else's. Why? Because your emotions are like training wheels – once you can spot them in yourself, you'll be better at spotting them in your parents.

QUICK DRILL

Answer YES, SOMETIMES, or NO

? | I can tell when I'm feeling happy, sad, or mad.

? | When I get upset, I know something that helps me calm down.

? | I notice when a friend or family member looks upset.

? | I can explain how I feel to someone using words.

➡ **Spy Tip:** Understanding yourself first makes it easier to crack the parent code.

SPY RANK UNLOCKED

ROOKIE OBSERVER

You've completed your first spy mission!

- You cracked the mystery of parent brains (with their To-Do Lists, Worry Clouds, and Love Bubbles).
- You matched emotions to facial expressions like a real detective.
- You practiced spotting your own feelings with a spy training drill.

That means you've earned your very first spy rank: **Rookie Observer.**

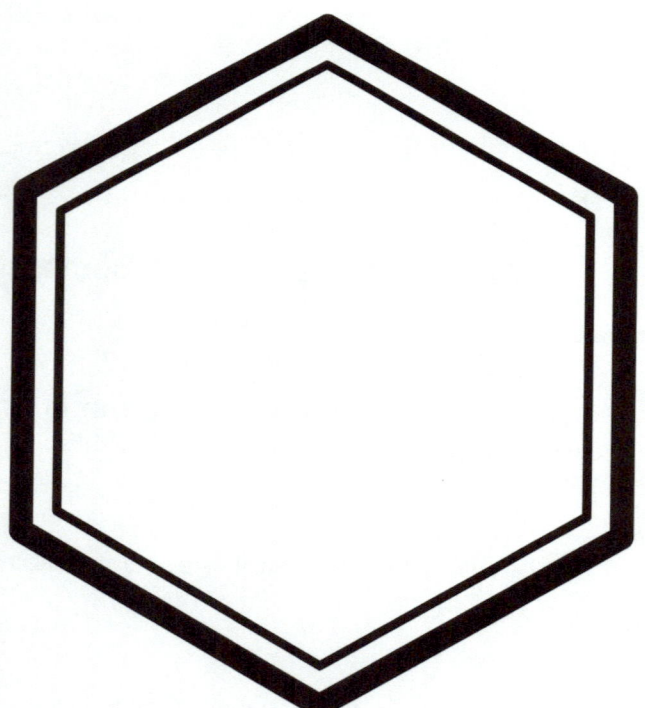

DESIGN YOUR ROOKIE OBSERVER BADGE

FEELINGS IN
DISGUISE

MISSION BRIEFING

Parents don't always show their true feelings on the outside. Stress, fear, tiredness, or even love can wear a disguise. **Your mission is to learn how to spot what's really going on beneath the surface.**

CLUES & EVIDENCE

Stress in Disguise

 Looks like yelling, grumpiness, or snapping over little things.

 Translation: Their backpack of responsibilities is overflowing.

Fear in Disguise

 Looks like lots of rules or saying "no" more often.

 Translation: They're really just worried about keeping you safe.

Exhaustion in Disguise

 Looks like sighing, zoning out, or not paying attention.

 Translation: Their brain is running on "low battery."

Love in Disguise

 Looks like too many questions, reminders, or rules.

 Translation: Even when it seems annoying, it's actually love popping through.

Frustration in Disguise

 Looks like: pacing around, groaning, or muttering under their breath.

 Translation: Something didn't go the way they hoped, and it's driving them bananas.

 **Wrap-Up:** Every disguise is just a clue. The real detective skill is spotting the hidden feeling underneath.

CASE FILE ACTIVITY:

BECOME A MOOD DETECTIVE

Sometimes grown-up feelings wear masks. Look at the clues. Which hidden feeling do you think is really behind the disguise?

Spy Tip: When you see a disguise, don't take it personally. Step back and ask: "What feeling could be hiding here?" That's how master detectives crack the code.

1. Mom says "No" three times in a row about going outside. Hidden Feeling: _____
2. Dad sighs loudly and stares at the floor after work. Hidden Feeling: _____
3. Grandma reminds you for the fifth time to grab a jacket. Hidden Feeling: _____
4. Your parent snaps about spilled juice, even though it's not a big mess. Hidden Feeling: _____

THE DISGUISE DECODER WHEEL

Every great spy needs a decoder tool. Use this one to match the outside behavior (the disguise) with the hidden feeling (the truth).

Step 1: Divide the circle into 4 slices like a pizza.
Step 2: In each slice, write one outside behavior
Step 3: Now write the hidden feeling behind it in the same slice
Step 4: Color each slice a different color and give your decoder wheel a spy name!

 **Spy Tip:** When you can decode the disguise, you see the truth – and that's how real detectives crack the toughest cases.

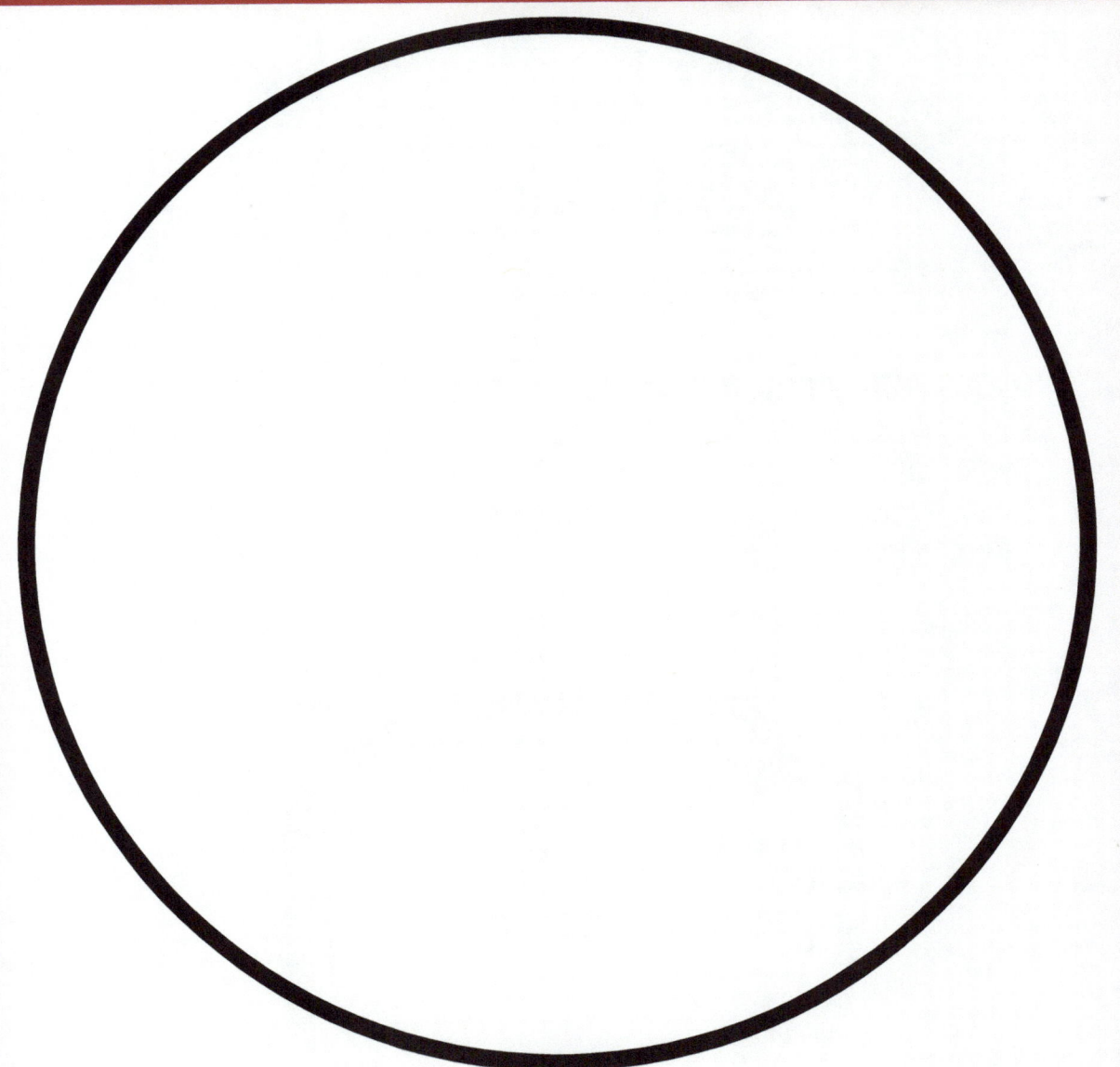

OUTSIDE BEHAVIOR

- Snapping or yelling
- Saying "no" a lot
- Sighing and zoning out
- Asking too many questions

HIDDEN FEELING

- Exhaustion
- Fear
- Love
- Stress

SPY RANK UNLOCKED

MOOD DETECTIVE

You've mastered a new set of spy skills!

- You spotted how stress, fear, exhaustion, love, and frustration can wear disguises.
- You learned to look past the outside behavior and uncover the hidden feelings inside.

That means you've earned your next spy rank: **Mood Detective.**

DESIGN YOUR MOOD DETECTIVE BADGE

RULES RULES RULES!

MISSION BRIEFING

If you think your parents have a rule for everything... you're not wrong! But here's the secret: rules are usually codes in disguise. **Your mission in this chapter is to crack those codes and figure out what rules really mean.**

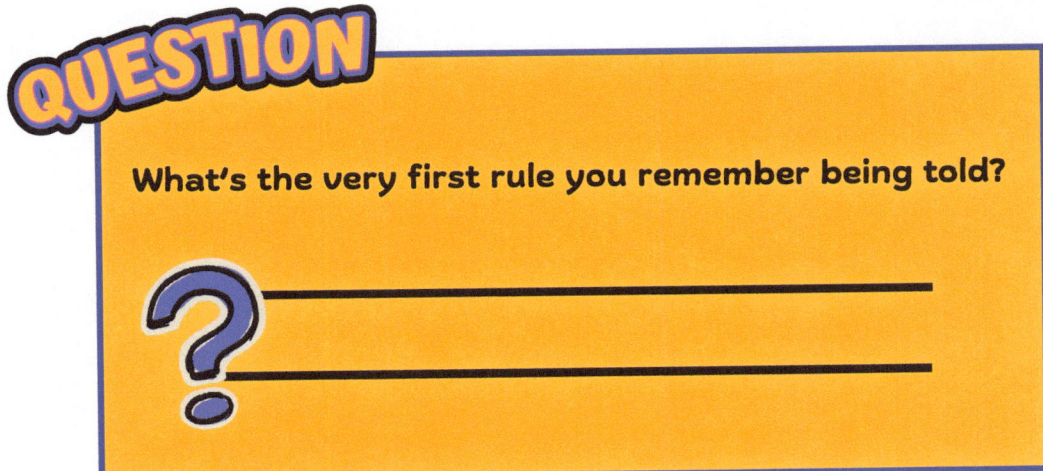

QUESTION

What's the very first rule you remember being told?

? _____
_____

CLUES & EVIDENCE

Rules usually fall into three top-secret categories:

SAFETY RULES

Keep you from danger.

Example: "Look both ways before crossing the street."

RESPONSIBILITY RULES

Teach you how to take care of yourself and your stuff.

Example: "Do your homework before screen time."

GROWTH RULES

Help you become a kind, smart, capable person.

Example: "Say thank you when someone gives you something."

CASE FILE ACTIVITY:

BECOME A RULE DECODER

Think about the rules in your house. Write one in each box below, then crack the code: is it a Safety Rule, Responsibility Rule, or Growth Rule?

Spy Tip: When you know what kind of rule it is, it feels less bossy and more like a clue about how your parent's mind works.

RULES

CATEGORY: _____

RULE:
_____
_____
_____

CATEGORY: _____

RULE:
_____
_____
_____

CATEGORY: _____

RULE:
_____
_____
_____

CATEGORY: _____

> **RULE:**
> _____
> _____
> _____

CATEGORY: _____

> **RULE:**
> _____
> _____
> _____

CATEGORY: _____

> **RULE:**
> _____
> _____
> _____

SPY RANK UNLOCKED

RULE DECODER

You've mastered a new set of spy skills!

- You discovered that rules are really secret codes about safety, responsibility, and growth.
- You practiced cracking your own house rules to reveal the meaning behind them.

That means you've earned your very first spy rank: **Rule Decoder.**

DESIGN YOUR RULE DECODER BADGE

HOW TO HEAR MORE YES!

MISSION BRIEFING

Every spy knows: timing, strategy, and evidence can make or break a mission. The same goes for asking parents for something you want. **Your mission: learn the secret formula that turns more "no" into "yes."**

QUESTION

If you could get a "YES" to anything right now, what would you ask for?

? _____

_____

YES!

 **CLUES & EVIDENCE**

The 3 P's of getting to

① Plan

Think before you ask. Is your parent busy, tired, or distracted? Wait for a better moment.

② Prove

Show you're responsible. Keep your word on little things, and parents will trust you with bigger things.

③ Promise

Explain how you'll handle it. Add a solution that makes parents feel safe saying yes.

Example: "If you let me have a sleepover, I promise to clean my room and finish homework first."

CASE FILE ACTIVITY:
THE YES MAP

Write down something you want to ask your parent for. Then use the 3 P's to strengthen your case.

Spy Tip: The best detectives know: a "yes" isn't luck – it's strategy.

strategy

THE YES MAP

What do you want to ask for?

PLAN

When is the best time to ask?

PROVE

How will you show you're responsible?

PROMISE

What will you do to make it fair?

Does this lead to → **YES**

SPY RANK UNLOCKED

NEGOTIATION AGENT

You've mastered a new set of spy skills!

- You learned that "no" isn't always final – it's just waiting for the right approach.
- You discovered the secret 3 P's – Plan, Prove, and Promise – that help turn "no" into "yes."

That means you've earned your very first spy rank: **Negotiation Agent.**

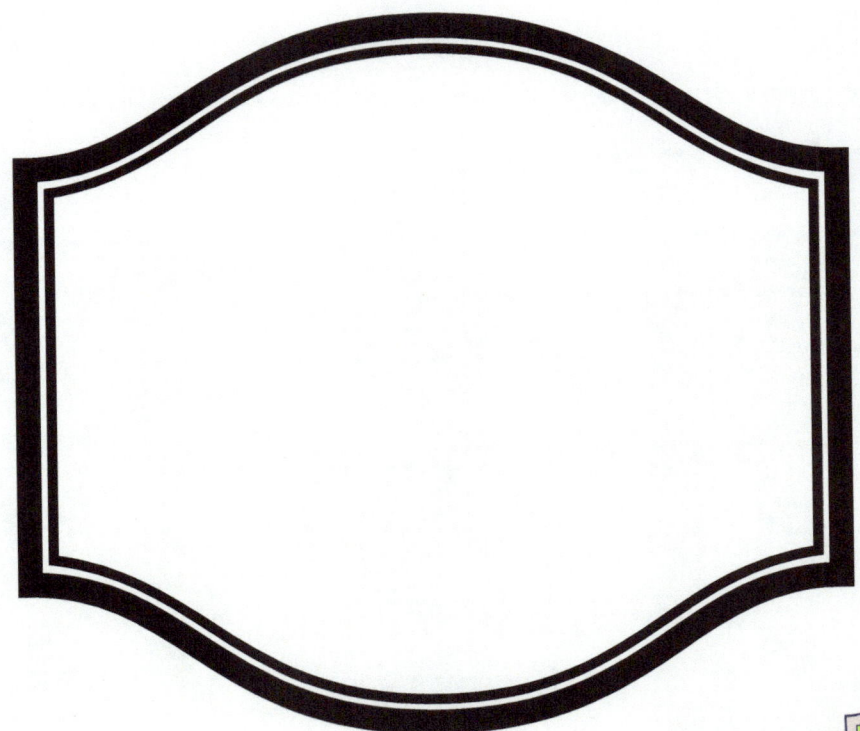

DESIGN YOUR NEGOTIATION AGENT BADGE

PARENTS WERE ONCE KIDS TOO!

 **MISSION BRIEFING**

Here's a shocking piece of spy intel: every parent was once... a kid! That means they played, laughed, made mistakes, and got into trouble – just like you.

Your mission: uncover what your parents were like when they were your age.

SPY CHALLENGE

Close your eyes and picture your parent as a kid. What do you see — braces? pigtails? a skateboard?
Now get ready to compare your guess with the real story.

 **CLUES & EVIDENCE**

Parents don't just seem like they've always been grown-ups – they actually have a whole kid history! They had favorite games, funny mistakes, and secret dreams, just like you.

Case File Notes:

- They had to follow rules (and probably broke a few).
- They had homework and chores to do.
- They had teachers they liked – and some they didn't.
- They sometimes felt nervous about fitting in with friends.
- They dreamed about their future, the same way you do now.

Remember: parents don't always share those stories right away. But the clues are there if you ask the right questions.

CASE FILE ACTIVITY:
PARENT TIME MACHINE

Interview your parent, grandparent, or another grown-up about their childhood. Write or draw their answers in the time machine.

Spy Tip: Every parent has a kid-version hiding inside. When you learn their story, you understand the choices they make today.

PARENT TIME MACHINE

Favorite Game

_____
_____

Biggest Fear

_____
_____

Rule They Hated Most

_____
_____

Funniest Memory

_____
_____

Dream For The Future

_____
_____

SPY RANK UNLOCKED
TIME-TRAVEL SLEUTH

You've leveled up your spy skills!

- You discovered that parents were once kids too – with their own fears, rules, and dreams.
- You cracked open the past to see the kid-version of your parent.

That means you've earned your very first spy rank: **Time-Travel Sleuth.**

DESIGN YOUR TIME-TRAVEL SLEUTH BADGE

CRACKING THE LOVE CODE

MISSION BRIEFING

Here's a secret spy file you didn't know existed: parents have their own love language. That's the special code they use to show how much they care. They may not always say "I love you" the way you expect – but they show it in ways that are just as powerful. **Your mission: figure out which love is your parent's secret code.**

SPY DISCOVERY

A language is just a way people share messages. Some languages use words, like English or Spanish. Others use pictures, like emojis 🙂🎉. And sometimes, actions are a language too — like a smile or a high-five.

CHAPTER 6

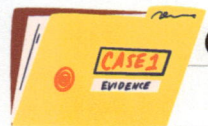

CLUES & EVIDENCE

Parents have their own love language – a special code for how they show you they care.

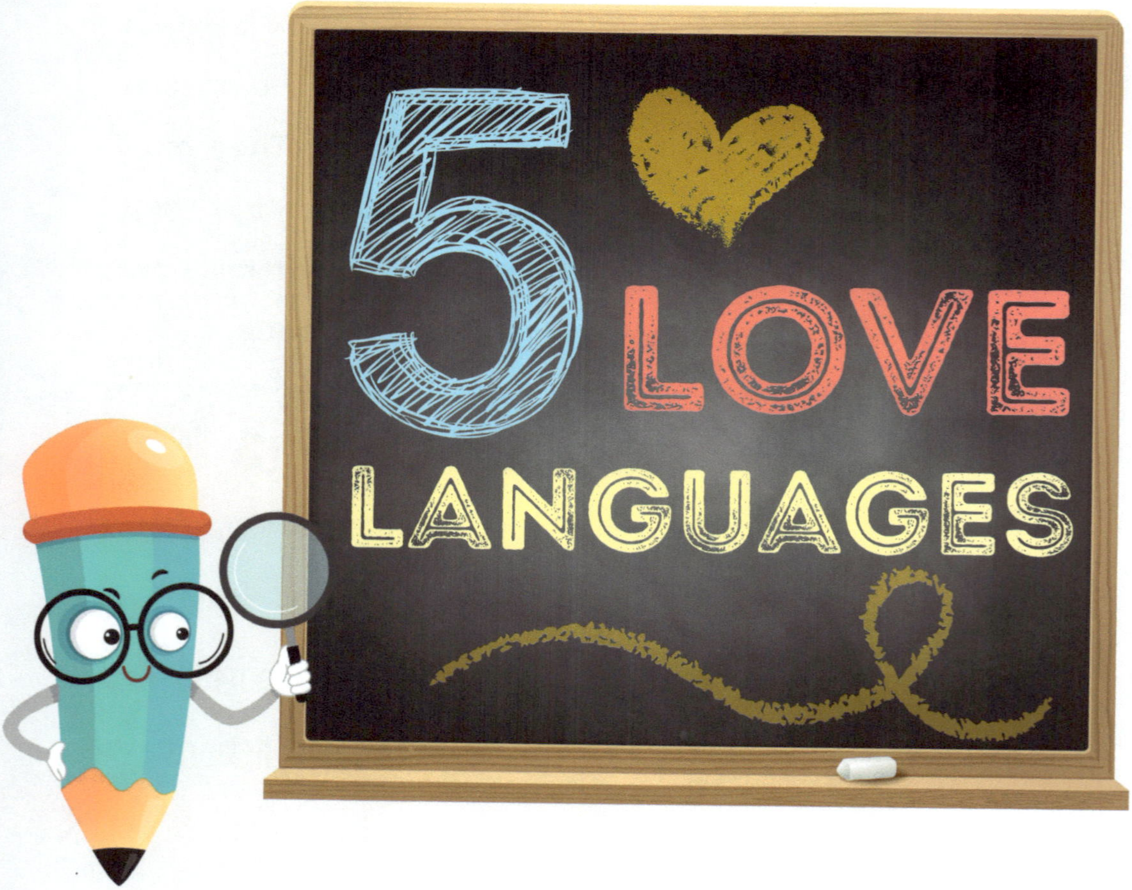

THE 5 LOVE LANGUAGES

Words of Affirmation

Love sounds like: "I'm proud of you," "You're awesome," or "Good job!"

Acts of Service

Love looks like: packing your lunch, helping with homework, or fixing your bike.

Gifts

Love shows up as: a surprise treat, a special toy, or a note in your backpack.

Quality Time

Love feels like: playing a board game together, reading a story, or going for a walk.

Physical Touch

Love comes through: hugs, high-fives, shoulder squeezes, or snuggles on the couch.

CASE FILE ACTIVITY:

DECODE THE LOVE LANGUAGE

Gather the evidence and crack the code. Match the clues that sound like your parent.

Spy Tip: Even if your parent doesn't say "I love you" all the time, their actions might be shouting it. Real spies know how to read the hidden code.

Do they say "I'm proud of you?"   **Acts of Service**

Do they help with chores or projects?   **Physical Touch**

Do they give little surprises?   **Quality Time**

Do they plan family time?   **Words of Affirmation**

Do they hug you often?   **Gifts**

SPY RANK UNLOCKED

LOVE CODE SPECIALIST

You've completed another spy mission!

- You discovered the 5 hidden ways parents show love.
- You practiced decoding the love language in your own family.

That means you've earned your very first spy rank: **Love Code Specialist.**

DESIGN YOUR LOVE CODE SPECIALIST BADGE

WHEN GROWN-UPS MESS UP

MISSION BRIEFING

Even the best spies mess up a mission sometimes – and parents do too. They might yell when they're stressed, forget a promise, or blame you for something that wasn't your fault.

Your mission: learn how to handle mistakes without letting them break the family team.

Detectives know: mistakes always leave clues. The real mission isn't about catching the mistake – it's about figuring out how to respond.

 **CLUES & EVIDENCE**

Parents aren't perfect. They make mistakes just like kids do.

Case File Notes:

➡ Stress overload: too many responsibilities can make parents snap faster than usual. (Think of it like too many tabs open on a computer!)

➡ Misunderstandings happen: parents don't always see the whole story and might jump to the wrong conclusion.

➡ Broken promises: sometimes life gets in the way, even when parents mean well.

➡ Apologies matter: just like kids, parents should say "I'm sorry" when they mess up.

Your reaction is power: calm words and forgiveness can turn mistakes into a chance to grow closer.

CASE FILE ACTIVITY:
SPY RESPONSE DRILL

Even the best detectives need a plan for when things go wrong. Read each situation. Then write how you could respond like a calm spy.

EXAMPLE

? **Situation:** Your parent spills water on the floor and gets frustrated.

Spy Response: Grab a towel and say, "I'll help clean it up – accidents happen." **!**

Spy Tip: When a grown-up messes up, your calm reaction is like a secret power. It can turn anger into understanding.

Your parent yells because they think you lost their keys, but then they find them in their own bag.

Your parent forgets to sign a permission slip you needed for school.

Your parent promises to play a game with you but gets stuck on a work call.

SPY RANK UNLOCKED

FORGIVENESS AGENT

You've leveled up your spy skills!

- You discovered that parents make mistakes, just like kids do.
- You practiced handling mess-ups with calm words and forgiveness.

That means you've earned your next spy rank: **Forgiveness Agent.**

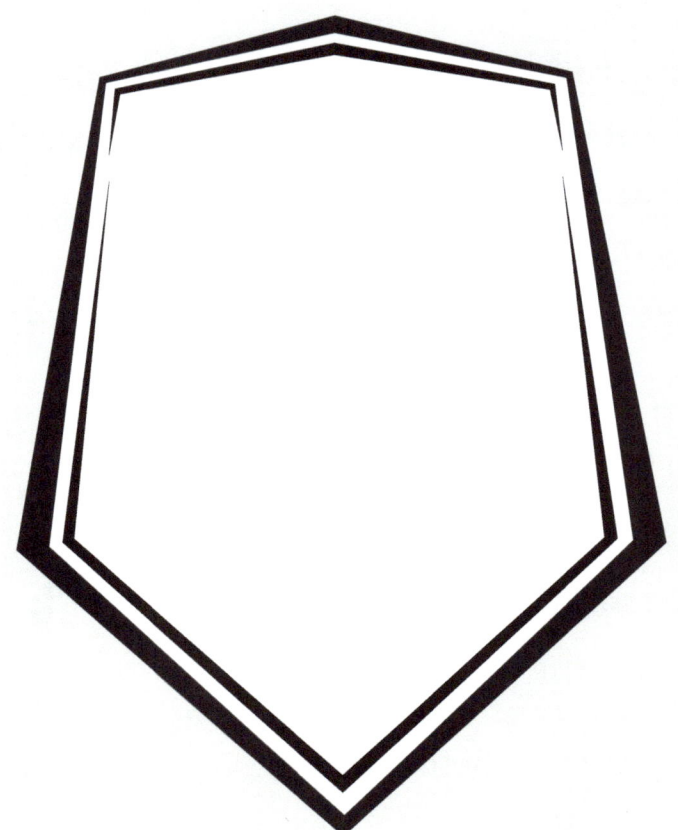

DESIGN YOUR FORGIVENESS AGENT BADGE

YOU CAN BE A MIND READER!
(SORT OF)

MISSION BRIEFING

Congratulations, agent – you've unlocked a new spy gadget: Detective X-Ray Glasses! No, they don't actually let you see inside someone's head... but they do help you spot clues on the outside. A frown, crossed arms, or even silence can reveal what a person is really feeling.

YOUR MISSION

Practice using your new gadget to pick up on hidden feelings before a single word is spoken.

 **CLUES & EVIDENCE**

Your Detective X-Ray Glasses can spot clues everywhere – faces, voices, and actions all tell a story. Here are the clues that help you crack the case of hidden feelings.

Case File Notes:

- **Faces tell stories.** Eyebrows, eyes, and mouths are like secret code symbols.

- **Body language speaks.** Crossed arms = closed off. Slumped shoulders = tired or sad.

- **Tone is a clue**. A sharp voice may mean stress. A quiet voice may mean worry.

- **Actions reveal feelings.** Slamming doors, pacing, or smiling big are all signs.

- **Context matters.** A frown in a video game is different from a frown at school.

TOP SECRET

Remember the **Worry Clouds** and **Love Bubbles** from Chapter 1? Your Detective X-Ray Glasses can spot them too!

A parent full of **Worry Clouds** might pace the room, tap their foot, or speak in a rushed tone.

Hidden Feeling: **stress or worry.**

A parent full of **Love Bubbles** might smile big, ask lots of questions about your day, or lean in close while you talk.

Hidden Feeling: **love and pride.**

Earlier clues become new evidence when you look carefully.

CASE FILE ACTIVITY:

X-RAY GLASSES PRACTICE

Slip on your imaginary Detective X-Ray Glasses and study these situations. Write what the hidden feeling might be.

Spy Tip: Mind-reading isn't magic – it's just careful observation. The more you practice, the sharper your detective powers become.

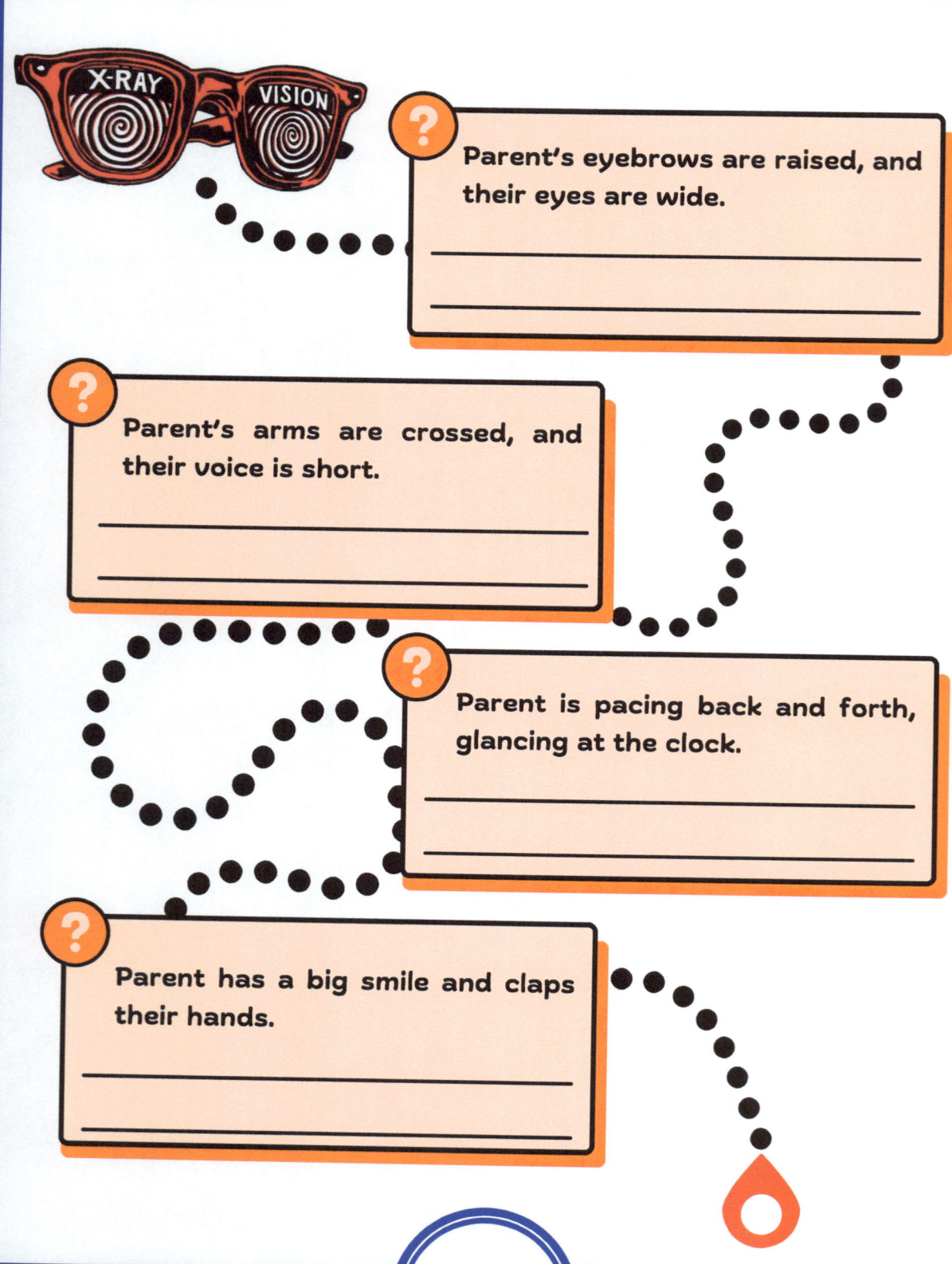

Parent's eyebrows are raised, and their eyes are wide.

_____

_____

Parent's arms are crossed, and their voice is short.

_____

_____

Parent is pacing back and forth, glancing at the clock.

_____

_____

Parent has a big smile and claps their hands.

_____

_____

SPY RANK UNLOCKED

EMPATHY EXPERT

You've mastered a new set of spy skills!

- You discovered how faces, voices, and actions reveal hidden feelings.
- You practiced using your Detective X-Ray Glasses to observe emotions like a pro.

That means you've earned your very first spy rank: **Empathy Expert.**

DESIGN YOUR EMPATHY EXPERT BADGE

FINAL MISSION!

CODE

MISSION BRIEFING

Agent, you've made it to your final mission. Along the way, you've cracked codes about rules, disguises, worry clouds, love bubbles, and even body language.

Now it's time to put all your detective skills together and finally complete your case: **understanding parents better.**

CRACKED

 **CLUES & EVIDENCE**

Case File Notes:

✳ You learned to spot the hidden feelings behind grown-up moods.

✳ You cracked the secret codes in their rules and decisions.

✳ You discovered that parents were once kids too.

✳ You decoded the love language that shows how they care.

✳ You practiced forgiveness when mistakes happen.

✳ You powered up your X-Ray Glasses to read body language and tone.

All those clues worked together to reveal the truth: parents aren't perfect, but they are always on your side.

CASE FILE ACTIVITY:
THE FINAL REPORT

Every great spy writes a debrief to capture what they've learned. Fill out your final report to close the case.

Spy Tip: This mission is complete, but your spy skills will keep helping you every day.

REPORT

One thing I understand about parents now that I didn't before:

REPORT

A clue I spotted in my parent that surprised me:

REPORT

One thing I'll try to do differently with my parent now:

REPORT

A spy skill I will keep using in real life is:

MISSION DEBRIEF AGENT GRADUATION

Congratulations, Agent! You've cracked every code, solved every case, and leveled up your spy skills. Along the way, you discovered:

- Parents have Worry Clouds, Love Bubbles, and disguises just like any mystery.
- Rules, mistakes, and moods all carry secret messages you can decode.
- Parents may not be perfect, but their love is always part of the story.

Your biggest discovery? That you are smart, capable, and ready to keep using these spy skills every day.

Mission Status: COMPLETE.

Agent Rank: MASTER CODE CRACKER.

But remember – spies never stop learning. Keep watching, keep asking questions, and keep decoding. The adventure continues...

AGENT GRADUATION

THIS CERTIFIES THAT

 _____

HAS COMPLETED
CRACKING THE PARENT CODE!
WELCOME TO THE RANK OF

MASTER CODE CRACKER

TOP SECRET

Also Available From Brenda D. Proctor

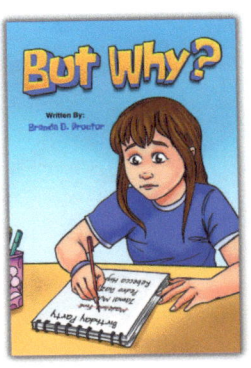

brendadproctorbooks.com

www.ingramcontent.com/pod-product-compliance
Lightning Source LLC
Chambersburg PA
CBHW041429120626
46547CB00002B/146